Ticcing My Way Through Life

BRITNEY WOLF

EduMatch
PUBLISHING

Contents

Dedication

To my parents, grandma, and my husband
Thank you for believing in me, never letting me quit, and loving every part of me. Without you, this wouldn't be possible.

To my Pappap who is no longer with us,
I did it! This is for you.

Introduction

"*Flick your wrist, now twist it in circles, flick your wrist, do it again, now with the other hand, at the same time. No, that wasn't right, do it again. Now slam your hand on the table, faster, faster, AGAIN.*"

These are the commands my brain often shouts at me as my body controls what I do, not the other way around. Even when it feels complete, it comes again.

"*Flick your wrist, now contract your stomach, in, out, in, out, hold your breath, but also breathe at the same time.*"

"What did they say? Was that important? I can't keep up with this meeting."

"*Keep going, you're not doing it right. Grunt every time you pull your muscles in, I don't care if someone hears you.*"

"What did she just say? Is she talking to me? I hope no one can tell I'm doing this."

"*We're not done here, do it again, do it until I tell you to stop....*"

Welcome to my life.

CHAPTER 1

A Day in My Shoes

I wake up in the morning just like any other person. I groggily roll over, hit my alarm as my dogs, Izzy and Brooklyn, begin to lick my face with the excitement of eating and going outside. On a really good day, I am awake for roughly 10 minutes before I start to lose control. But, on a bad day, the tics start as soon as that alarm clock sounds...and don't stop until I'm back in bed and asleep.

The very first tic that greets me is with my feet. As I walk my dogs outside, my feet start to kick the ground—once on my right foot, then a circular motion on my left, then two quick kicks back on my right. After that, I start the tic all over again, but this time I start on the left because it has to be even. This continues while I make my way back into the house—kicking the whole time, wondering if anyone is up this early watching out of their windows while having their morning coffee.

"Do I think anyone cares what I'm doing at 6 am? Of course, they don't, but... what if they do...and what if they think I'm crazy...?"

Different objects and different ways of using my body can be a big trigger for me. When I sit down on my couch to eat my breakfast, I get this incredibly uncomfortable feeling all over my body. The urge starts as I feel the cushion of the couch pushing into the curve of my back. I begin to plead with myself to just get through breakfast without making a mess. I pull myself away from the couch to sit straight up, but it's too late and the need for a tic has already begun. The slamming begins. My lower back smacks into the couch, followed by my shoulders, and just like that, while barely awake at 6:30 am, I'm in the middle of a complex tic taking away what little energy I have. Even when I feel complete, it's only for a moment, because once is never enough. Then again, neither is doing it five, ten, or even twenty times. For as long as I live, the tics will never be "enough" to make them stop.

After slamming my way through breakfast, I finish my morning routine. I open my bathroom door, flip on the light, then tap it 4 times, one tap, one circular motion, then 2 quick taps again. The pattern has to be just right before I can get any further into the room. Sometimes this lasts only a few minutes. Sometimes I'm stuck in the doorway for 5 minutes or more. I brush my teeth, fix my hair, and get dressed— usually with no issues, but that depends on the day.

As I walk out of the bathroom, I tap where the doorknob meets the door—one tap, one circular motion, and then 2 quick taps (beginning to see a pattern?). This compulsion of mine is a friendly cohabitant of Tourette Syndrome, called OCD or Obsessive-Compulsive Disorder. That's the thing with Tourette Syndrome; it's never just tics. The tapping on the door and my light switch routine are just the beginning of my compulsions.

I wrap up my morning routine and jump in the car to drive to work. The concentration I have on the road, or the songs or podcasts on the radio, helps me to drive without too much concern. Tics with my eyes last a matter of seconds, but I blink hard while I drive and sometimes roll my eyes to the back of my head causing me to not focus on the road as I should.

My body constantly forces me to move in ways that it's not supposed to, and being in the car is no exception. If I can't do it, the tics just get worse and worse—causing me to have breathing practices in place while I'm driving, so I can attempt to pull myself out of it and calm my body down.

Although it doesn't happen often, there are days where I'm forced to call off work or ask my husband to drive me where I need to go because I'm scared that my tics could cause an accident. Those are the days where I beat myself up the most. I feel like I'm losing. I feel like I'm a burden to the ones I love.

I make my way to work, pulling into the same parking spot I find every morning. I press the button to shut off the engine, sit back, and take a deep breath. I instantly feel my ankle twist as I push it into the floor while pushing my back against the seat simultaneously. In between tics, I grab my glasses and my badge and open up the door to head into the building. I hear the birds chirping and the wind on my face while I kick my feet, or slide my feet/shoes across the pavement in a repetitive motion almost the whole time I walk through the parking lot. I try to contain it as much as possible as I walk through my building to avoid any possible stares from people who do not know that I have Tourette Syndrome.

All the tics I held in while walking through the building make their way out of my body once I get to my desk. I sign onto my computer and I instantly start clicking my mouse over and over again. Just having my hand on the mouse triggers me to start clicking and slamming my mouse down on my desk. This is extremely frustrating because of the sheer fact that there is no way I can do my job without holding and clicking on my mouse. So now I'm self-conscious about my co-workers having to listen to my incessant clicking all day long. I get worried that they will find my clicks annoying, especially if they don't understand why I'm doing it. I try to push through as best as possible, all while trying not to let my ticing and clicking get in the way of doing my job.

I click my way through the 8-9 hour day and go through the same process on my way home as I did in the morning. It's when I get home that the tics start to ramp up and come out in full force because of all the pent-up energy from work. All the movements that were kept inside throughout the workday start to make their way out of my system. My hands find doorknobs and light switches to tap. I kick my feet against each other and I start to slam my back on the couch. My facial and jaw tics take over while watching tv, causing headaches and jaw pain the following day. These are just a portion of some of the tics that happen after a day of trying to sit still in my office chair all day long, but there is always a variance in severity, and the type of tics my body decides to do.

After a day of losing control while trying to maintain a straight face and look "normal" to either my teachers, peers, managers, or coworkers, I become mentally drained. With each class or hour of my work day that passes by, my mind, body, and emotions are at a peak. This makes it difficult to focus with each tick of the clock and all I can think about is going back home where I can tic in peace. On the really bad days, my focus is nowhere to be found and all I can think about is what my body is making me do. I become self conscious about every little movement and constantly watching out of my peripherals to see if anyone is noticing what I've been doing all day or if they would even care if they did.

Exhaustion sets in by the time I'm ready to crawl into bed. I wish I could say this forces my tics to hit pause, but unfortunately, it's the exact opposite. I spent the day trying to be discreet, trying to drive safely, and getting to work on time, so everything that didn't happen throughout the day finds its way out of my body. The tics show up the same way every night. I kick my foot against the bottom of my other one four to five times in a row and then do it again with the opposite foot so they are both even and continue for a good five minutes on a good night. I usually don't do it "right" and have to start the pattern over again. It has to feel right in my brain for my tic to actually feel

4

complete and even then, it doesn't stop me from having to do it again. This tic is sometimes accompanied by others including slamming my knees together, and sometimes lifting my back off the bed, and then forcefully pushing it back down again. On bad nights, it can take a very long time for all my nightly tics to stop and it causes a lack of sleep, stress, and a much more tic-filled morning the next day. Exhaustion eventually finds me and I fall asleep until I begin the whole routine again the next morning.

ties came and went and my tics went with them. But, here I am typing this book while slamming my hands and fingers against the keyboard during and in between my sentences. My constant companion is still with me over 20 years later and continues to show up at the most inconvenient times in my life. I wasn't one of the "lucky" ones that got to grow out of Tourette Syndrome, but I am one of the lucky ones that gets to use this part of life to try and help other people and that's a pretty good trade if you ask me.

CHAPTER 5

Tics Through the Years

T he biggest question I have always been asked is "How do you tic?" Aside from being asked if I swear all the time, the two most common questions are what I do when I tic, and if it hurts when I do it. Well, I would be here all day if I listed EVERY single tic that I do, but I will highlight a few of the worst tics I've had over the years as well as the ones that I have most frequently today. It's important to remember that everyone who has Tourettes is different and we all have different movements or sounds that happen throughout the day or even years of our lives. Some fade away, old ones come back, and sometimes you can wake up one day with a brand-new tic. Every day is different for someone living with Tourette Syndrome, and those of us affected never know what kind of day it will be until it happens.

The worst and most pronounced tic that I can remember was flipping my head backward. I used to flip my head down, allowing all my hair to fall as if I was about to blow-dry or style it, and then flip it back up. If all my hair didn't fall over my head, I would have to repeat it. If I tripped over myself while it happened, I would have to do it again, each time with more force as if my body was punishing me for doing it "wrong" the first time. I would do this constantly and because of that, I suffered from a lot of neck and back pain and headaches. My neck would be sore daily and I would ask my mom to help rub out the kinks all the time. This tic was still prevalent on Halloween when my friends and I were trying to make a Halloween movie together. Being the great supporting friends that they were, they came up with the idea that in the movie I was going to be a dancer for Halloween, that way when I would flip my head/hair over and back up, it would look like I was playing my dancer role in our movie. Thankfully, this tic, for the most part, has faded away and I haven't had to think of clever ways to make it work in social situations. However, every once in a while, when I'm drying my hair with a towel after a shower or after swimming, it triggers my head to do it again, but nothing like before.

Another big tic that I had while growing up that I am *extremely* thankful I don't have anymore is straddle jumping. A straddle jump is a jump that is most often associated with cheerleaders and dancers. While in the air, both legs are extended straight out to each side. I think I had this tic because of my dance background. But, one Christmas Eve I was so excited, I was jumping all over my grandmother's house. The worst part was, I remember my body having to do it in the tightest of places. It was almost like it was some kind of game my mind was playing with me. Every time I went through a doorway (that my legs just barely fit through while doing a straddle jump), every time I hit that last step coming downstairs or walking down off of my Grandma's porch, it was a trigger for the tic to take over. Sometimes, I would have to crouch down and jump up from that position as if my body was winding up to expel the tic at full force. I have always **loved** Christmas and I still do, so whenever the Christmas season came around my tics would get a lot worse. It still happens to this day as an adult, because this is my favorite time of year, but thankfully that tic has yet to make another appearance in my life, and I hope it stays that way.

Nowadays, I tend to tic with my eyes, jaw, and neck a lot. My facial tics are amongst the ones that I'm more self-conscious about. I've gotten myself into some trouble on occasion from people thinking I was showing attitude and rolling my eyes at them. My eyes will roll so far to the back of my head that when they come back, my vision blurs momentarily and I feel pain throughout my entire eye. The aches that occur after the tic only cause more of a trigger to repeat it. In my body, feeling that tenderness increases the urge and need for my body to tic more. My eyes lead into more facial tics as it becomes more complex. I move my head in a circular motion along with stretching out my mouth jaw at the same time. Whichever direction my head goes, I always have to stretch my jaw in the opposite direction—I think for whatever reason, this makes my brain feel like everything is equaling itself out. I always thought that my body would get used to the movements so I wouldn't be as sore anymore after a day of high tic levels, but unfortunately, that is not always the case for me. Complex facial and head tics always lead to jaw and neck pain and depending on the complexity or intensity, tension headaches stemming from the back of my head where it meets my neck.

Another set of movements that are still dominant to this day are done with my hands and my feet. When I'm writing or doing something specific with my hands, I have to stop what I'm doing to kind of flick my wrists back and forth until it feels right. I used to just flick my wrists, but over time the tic grew into more of a complex tic, just like they did with my head. I began to rotate my hands into a circular motion, my right hand going clockwise, with my left hand going counterclockwise, and then once they come full circle, I flick my wrists twice to the sides. The worst part about my tics for me is that every time I finish it, for a split second it feels right—as if I won't ever have to do it again. When I do it right, it feels complete, and as silly as it sounds, a part of me thinks "maybe that was it, maybe my body did what it wanted one final time and I'll finally stop doing this." Only that's not what happens at all. Actually, I barely have enough time to even have that full thought run through my head before my body is doing it again.

Moving down the body, come to my stomach tics. My stomach tics were the first ones I noticed and still happen to this day quite often. This is why people tell me that they don't even realize that I have it because I'm usually ticcing with my stomach and they can't see it. I move my stomach muscles in and out, and my fingers usually move around in a circular motion at the same time (you'll notice that the circular motion with my fingers and hands is a popular move with my body). When the tic is at its highest intensity, I grunt with each stomach movement—I breathe in while pulling my muscles towards my back, and then grunt quietly two times. This will continue until I can't breathe anymore. I'm always trying to find ways to tic discreetly, so that I don't get asked about it or to make the people around me more comfortable. Even though I know I can't control it, and I know that it's not my job to make everyone else comfortable, I still try to.

When I tic with my feet, it's usually when I'm walking since I'm obviously using my feet to get there; that's the part of the body that gets triggered to move in ways I wished it didn't. I will be in the store with my husband, and I have to stop in the middle of the aisle to kick or stomp on the ground. I slide my feet on the floor in front of me and then kick the ground two times, and as always, this gets repeated on the other side for the tic to be complete. Sometimes I will be stopped in the middle of a store for 5 or 10 minutes before I can get the energy to pull myself out of it. Ticcing in public, as I do with my kicking tic, is always one of the harder ones. I always wonder if it's going to cause a scene, or if that particular day will be the day when someone has a problem with it or mocks me publicly. People are unpredictable and can be pretty unkind when it comes to things they don't understand, so it's always a worry in the back of my mind.

I wish I could say that this is where the tics stop—that I only tic with those parts of my body, but I can't. Tourette Syndrome is a rollercoaster I never wanted to ride. I wake up every single day not knowing what's going to happen or how bad it's going to be. It doesn't hurt all the time and sometimes I don't feel the pain until the next day, but it does hurt. With the physical pain comes the toll it takes on my mentality and my emotions. A day spent ticcing non-stop is known to put me in a dark place mentally and emotionally. These days leave me not feeling like myself and leave me wanting to be different or "normal." No one knows what no control means until they feel their entire body moving on their own with no intentions of stopping. I get so tired and angry because all I want is to just sit down and relax, but for me relaxing doesn't always come easy. What I want from my body and what it wants to do are two entirely different things.

CHAPTER 6

What Does a Tic Feel Like?

There are a lot of different ways a person can try and explain what having a tic feels like, but I can promise you almost every single person will tell you "it's hard to explain" or that it's flat out impossible. It's funny because you would think the one thing you do every single day, every hour of the day, would be something you could define effortlessly. Although I do it constantly, defining it perfectly is very difficult, but I'm going to attempt it anyway to give those reading without the disorder a glimpse inside my body when it happens. Sometimes it starts as an urge or a feeling I get within my body, and other times—most of the time—there is no warning as to when the tics are going to show themselves. If and when I do feel like I am about to tic, I can feel it throughout my entire body. I feel it from my head down through my stomach almost as if it's a premonition; it's a feeling that is almost indescribable and doesn't go away until I'm forced to give in. It's a constant battle inside my head and my body telling me to move, while all I can think about is wanting to sit still.

Throughout the years, the motions with my head and my neck have changed a lot. A lot of it consists of tilting my head back or to the side as if I'm stretching. I hear my neck cracking every time I tilt my head back and feel the strain every time I pull it to the side. Even though most of the time it doesn't hurt during the tic itself, it causes a lot of pain and muscle fatigue later that day and the days following. Sometimes it's the tic in itself, but most of the time for me, it's the repetition of body movements and the constant ticcing that hurts. There could be days, weeks, or even months on end where I tic with the same body part, or there could be times where I do a different tic every day and that is what determines how sore my body will be from all the movements. After days of ticcing with my neck, it becomes very sensitive, and the chances of me pulling a neck muscle grows stronger. Sometimes I pull a muscle just by looking to the side because of how sensitive the muscles become after my tics and the pain shoots up to where my neck starts to meet the back of my head.

As I said before, tics can come and go. I can tic a certain way for months and one day it will disappear. At the same time, one day I might tic in a way that I never have before. Whether I "feel" the urge before it happens or if my body just starts moving, the nearly indescribable feeling is always the same. I feel it from somewhere deep inside; I begin to feel a sensation in my stomach, and something else takes control of me. I can't talk or breathe while a tic is in motion and my heart rate starts to race a bit as my body forces it all out. I never know how long each one will last or how many times I will have to do it. I just sit there hoping it won't end in a panic attack or what a lot of us with Tourette Syndrome call a Tic Attack where I zone out and tic with my entire body all at once. These can sometimes be a little like a panic or anxiety attack, except with tics. Every once in a while I can feel it coming on, when I'm not ticcing the way my body needs me too. I start to tic faster and more intensely; my breath shortens and everything else around me no longer exists. Then there are the moments where they happen out of nowhere. No matter if I feel it coming or it comes out of nowhere, tic attacks are really scary experiences for me.

To the average person reading this who knows what it's like to

26

make the decision to move your body, this may sound strange, but to us in the TS community, it's just another day in our lives. Sometimes I try to explain it as if someone has hiccups. Most people know the routine; you hiccup once, usually at the most inopportune time, and hope the hiccups end quickly. Sometimes the hiccup can be small and discreet; other times (if your hiccups are anything like mine) hiccups can be loud, obnoxious ones that can make the whole grocery store curious as to what you just did (yes, that actually happened to me). But, the point is, you don't know what your body is going to do next. You don't know when they are going to go away, or how they will sound or feel one minute to the next. Sometimes they can be painful, embarrassing even, and sometimes no one in the room may even know you have them. In my opinion, the hiccups are one of the closest comparisons that I could come up with for someone to have a slight understanding of what a tic feels like on a daily basis for a person living with Tourette Syndrome. The difference being, I cannot simply drink a glass of water or hold my breath to make my tics go away. I can only hope to get through the day the best that I can.

Another good explanation of what a tic feels like or what the urge is like would be for the average person feeling a sneeze coming on. Only there are still differences in the experience. You begin to feel the tickle in your nose. I begin to feel the urge to move my stomach. You start to look at the light because one time you were told that it would make you sneeze. I try my best to do everything to stop mine. You begin to feel your breath start to escape you as your nose prepares for the sneeze. I feel my urges grow stronger in my stomach, now through my hands and feet while I know it's about to happen. Your sneeze comes out and you instantly feel better. I finally let my tic out and my stomach contracts, my shoulders hunch over, and my hands form a half-clenched position. Everyone around you says "Bless You" and moves on. I'm afraid to even look up because I'm afraid someone around me will be staring, wondering "what is wrong with her?" The difference is, everyone thinks what you did was normal, but I have to explain myself and worry about how I will be treated because of it.

I won't ever be able to give the perfect description so that those outside of the community understand. But, everyday I try my best to explain what it feels like in my body while a tic is happening. Sometimes it can be tiring having to constantly explain myself or worry about what's going to happen when I tic. But, I'll never stop trying to spread awareness because the more we speak up and speak out, the more we normalize it. Maybe explaining how a tic feels won't do that in itself, but every single detail can help. To get people to understand us, we have to put them in our shoes and try to get them to feel the way we feel as best we can—even for just a moment.

CHAPTER 7

Ticcing My Way Through School

Most of the time, concentrating on what was in front of me is what got me through the day. But, when the bad days found me, concentrating on anything in front of me, or whatever the teacher was saying, was almost impossible. I dealt with this every day throughout my education not knowing what kind of day I was going to have, or what kind of 40-minute struggle it was going to be. I could go through one class with zero issues and then in the next feel uncomfortable or get triggered and tic uncontrollably.

I remember the bad days vividly. It felt like everything around me kept moving on, while I was sitting there struggling internally, and no one could see it, no one understood it, and no one could make it stop...least of all me. Those were the days where I doubted myself, where I pleaded with myself just to make it through without causing disruption and without anyone else staring at me as I flicked my head back as discreetly as possible (and trust me, that tic was never actually discreet). I hoped that even if the tics fired up, maybe my teachers would be understanding and let me do what I needed to do to calm myself down. For the most part, that was the case. And because teachers didn't know what Tourette Syndrome really was, or how to handle it, they pretty much let me do what I needed to do.

Although the empathy was there for the most part, it didn't take away from my inability to focus in the classroom while I was fighting a battle no one knew anything about. I constantly felt like I was living in a world where I had to hide a part of me— the biggest part of me, just to make everyone else feel comfortable.

I remember walking into class and sitting in the tan desk, with a red or blue chair connected to it. I can see my colored notebooks sitting on top of the desk with my color-coordinated folder and book cover, because everything had to match and be perfect. I put the books I don't need in the basket under my seat and wait to see what the next 40 minutes has in store for me.

I open my notebook and see those empty blue lines staring back at me. I put my pencil on the paper. The tics started instantly. Tapping the paper, retracing my letters, writing the same letters or numbers over and over again, faster and faster. Eventually, I found myself scribbling out everything I was trying to write down. The teacher kept going and I found myself trying to write faster and faster, just to catch up. I tried to focus on what my teacher was telling me while battling this monster inside my own brain. The tics kept coming, as my heartbeat grew faster with each click of the clock, wondering why or how time could possibly move so slow.

"Is everyone noticing what I am doing?"

"Does the teacher see me?"

"If she does... is she going to believe me when I tell her that I can't make it stop?"

Retaining anything the teacher said to me was merely a dream on those days. On those bad days, I had no choice but to give in. Those were the days where it killed me to admit, even as a child, that sometimes it was just too much.

Normally, I don't suppress my tics around other people, especially now that I am older. But, I don't think there is a person out there with Tourette Syndrome who hasn't gotten at least a little self-conscious about what the people around them are thinking when it happens. The classroom was probably the biggest struggle for my battle of whether or not to let my tics out or if I should try and suppress them, for as long as it was possible. I knew what kind of evening would be in store for me after a day of suppression, but as a child who was afraid of getting bullied for something out of my control, it was hard to decide which option was worse. Allow myself to possibly get teased by those around me or mask and try to hide the tics which would lead to an evening of nothing but nonstop movement until I closed my eyes?

I glanced up at the students in the room, some engaged in the lesson, others writing notes to their friends, some sleeping, and others trying to get on their phones without the teacher noticing. Sometimes I grew envious of those around me, sitting in the classroom, having complete control over what their body was doing. *"How did that feel? What is it like to always know what's coming next?"* I wondered, thinking that I must be the only one feeling so anxious and embarrassed just by sitting in a room.

Why did I have to try and be considerate of how other people felt when no one wanted to try and understand and be considerate of how hard it was for me? All those times of attempting to suppress my tics were all for them and they had no idea. Because sometimes it was just easier to not have to explain myself to everyone around me, especially in the moment. Sometimes it was just easier to deal with the consequences later. The trade-off was, if I successfully hid my tics, they would find their way out of me, in the next class, the hallway, the ride home, and or at night. I could suppress them and win the battle...but that didn't mean I won the war.

Thankfully, I had a pretty great school system where my peers were generally as understanding as they could be with something they knew nothing about. But that doesn't mean it wasn't hard. I grew up with the statistics showing that because I had Tourette Syndrome, school was going to be difficult for me. Parents are often told to not expect their children to do well in school or to not expect them to be honor students. The statistics weren't lying when they said it would be hard; it was near impossible to concentrate some days. But lucky for me, I never liked being told what I was and wasn't capable of. I was determined to show everyone that this disorder that took control over so much of my life wasn't going to take over my education too. I worked so hard and I tried to go above and beyond in everything that I did. I was a perfectionist at the core and it was my blessing and my curse. The blessing allowed me to be an honor student almost my entire life and the curse made it difficult to forgive myself during the times I missed the honor roll by just one class.

Sometimes thinking about those bad days in school can still make me tear up and can even trigger me to tic in the same way if I think about it too much. But then, I remember my teachers, the ones who showed an enormous amount of understanding and empathy. The teachers who let me tic peacefully and be myself. That is something I am so grateful for. The good days outweigh the bad days, but feeling as comfortable as I could on those bad days is what helped me make it through them.

Their understanding allowed me to be a student that excelled in the classroom, even with all the worries and anxiety that came with Tourette Syndrome. I didn't want to be a distraction, and I prided myself on being a good student. Because of that, negative, intrusive thoughts often filled my brain. I was proud of who I was because of Tourette Syndrome, but ticcing in public, especially in school, is still something that's difficult to do. You never know what people will say, if people will laugh, or worst of all for me, if people will even believe me....

Being a teenage student was hard enough, and throwing Tourette Syndrome into the mix brought it to a level most didn't know about.

Because of that, my teachers had the opportunity to make or break me. They could have made me hate school, but thanks to their compassion and understanding, I was the student that I knew I could be, even with odds against me. Unfortunately, I know this is not the same story that we all share.

Students everywhere are suffering every day in school. They are being kicked out of classrooms and being suspended by people they should be able to trust.. I was one of the lucky ones, but not everyone gets the experience that I had growing up. Tourette Syndrome is a weird and sometimes an unbelievable thing for those on the outside, but it's real and it's hard. It is so much more than what you see on the movie screen; it's something that truly affects people and makes life so much more difficult, especially throughout adolescence.

A student in the classroom with Tourette Syndrome, or similar disorders and disabilities, deserves not only respect but the inclusion and acceptance that every other student receives walking into their classrooms. It might take a little extra effort, but I promise you every ounce of effort you put into their learning experience will stay with them for the rest of their lives. In my eyes, a teacher's success is only as good as the connection they make with their students, long after they leave those four walls.

CHAPTER 8

The Teachers Who Made a Difference

After my diagnosis, there were a lot of statistics thrown my way about what my life would be like in and out of school. Doctors and research showed that things would most likely be pretty difficult for me through my schooling and that's all it took for me to want to prove all those statistics wrong. I knew just because that's how it was for some or even most students with Tourette Syndrome, that was not going to be me. I promised myself from that day forward that I would be the student no one anticipated that I would be. I'm not saying it was easy, because it wasn't. I'm also not saying that I had it as bad as a lot of people with Tourette Syndrome, because I didn't. However, that didn't mean that the added stress of papers, homework, tests, and grades didn't make my Tourettes go haywire.

A new school year always brought on different emotions for me. I was always excited to start school again because I was the kid that liked school growing up (at least until high school anyways). But with that excitement came anxiety about what the classroom would be like for me. I never really told a lot of people about my fears of the classroom because I didn't want anyone to worry and be concerned, but the worries were there. *"Do I have to tell my teachers, and if I do, will they even know what it is, will they believe me? Will my friends finally be fed up and embarrassed about being with the girl who moved weird? Will new students think of me as the weird girl with Tourette Syndrome?"* All kinds of questions would swirl through my mind which would cause the tics to get a little worse right before the school year started as well. All sorts of emotions would run through my body, making my tics go crazy, adding to the domino effect of my earlier stated questions about ticcing in front of people in the classroom.

Because of my fears of people staring or possibly making fun of me in the classroom, I always went with the approach of getting to them before they got to me. I figured if I was open and upfront about my disorder, and then, if they were still going to judge or make fun of me, they were the ones with a problem and not me. So, every year for as long as I could remember, any time I had the opportunity to write about or do a project on a subject of my choosing, I would always, without hesitation, pick Tourette Syndrome. I saw it as the perfect opportunity to teach my class (when they were projects to present in the classroom) and my teachers about my condition. Even though my tics were subconsciously suppressed for the most part in the classroom, that didn't mean they didn't find their way out, and I never wanted to be the disruptive kid in the room, so I wanted to tell everyone why my body might do things that seemed purposeful or funny. I wanted them to know I couldn't control it, no matter how much I tried. I would say that this tactic was successful about 90% of my time in school.

While most teachers were perceptive and believed me when my mom or I told them about my disorder, I could always tell that they didn't really know how to handle the situation as a whole. I would always be able to tell when an adult or anyone else around me either never heard of Tourette Syndrome before, or only ever knew it as a joke and never knew that it was a real thing that affected someone's life in a very serious way. It was weird, because they were the teacher, but there I was teaching them something that they knew nothing about. It made it slightly uncomfortable for me sometimes when I would have to be excused because I was ticcing and needed to take a lap around the school or go lay down in the nurse's office so that I could calm down. They would always say yes, but on occasion, their faces would show more concern than was necessary.

I remember one time I went to the nurse's office and just asked to sit there or lie down for a little bit and because she never experienced that kind of "illness" in her office before, she called my mom not knowing what to do. I didn't blame her for her concern, but the tone of voice she had when she called was a little different and you could tell she just had absolutely no idea what to do with me, even though I tried explaining to her that I was fine. I just needed some time to myself to calm my mind and breathe. I just needed some time where I knew there weren't eyes staring at me, wondering what I was going to do next.

Although my experience in school was rather uneventful, when I think back to that time and my tics, two specific scenarios and teachers always come to mind. One, in particular, being my art teacher in middle school. This teacher would always have us gather around his desk when we started a new project so he could show us the "right" way to draw, which was always insane in my mind. I always thought that there wasn't a right way to draw or make art, especially for a middle school student, but I guess not according to this teacher. On this particular day, I was the lucky student who got to stand right next to him while we were gathered around his giant gray, perfectly square desk. I remember seeing the other students standing around me, watching as his pencil hit the gridded paper showing us what our drawings were supposed to look like that day. I felt my best friend's arm rub up against mine by accident as there was only so much room for students to stand and that's when the tics started to happen. I'll never forget that look in his eye as he looked up at me over his glasses as if I was stupid or something and said, "Can you please just sit still?"

To this day, I still get that same sinking feeling in the pit of my stomach as I think back to that moment and type this story. I can feel every ounce of embarrassment, anxiousness, and the tears that threatened to come in front of all of my classmates. My best friend at the time, being as wonderful as she was, whispered to me with a worried look in her eye while asking "are you ticcing?" and I slowly nodded my head yes as I stared down at my feet and then back at the drawing on the table. I felt her grab my arm to let me know that she was there for me, a small moment that I'll never forget from her.

This particular teacher didn't know that I had Tourette Syndrome. It was just a teacher that we never had a chance to tell, and it was only a nine week art class that I didn't find necessary to bring up. You would think at that moment, I would have let him know about my disorder, but that look in his eye and the tone in his voice froze me. I didn't know what to say and I thought that he wouldn't have believed me even if I told him— so why even try to defend myself? This teacher wasn't known for being overly nice to students, at least not to most students, so it made more sense in my mind to just put my head down, blink back the tears, and get through the class.

My mother, on the other hand, was livid. She told me that if he didn't believe me she would have been in that school so fast with all my paperwork to prove it to him. But, I told her it didn't matter. I didn't want to cause more problems or make anything weird. I already didn't like art class because art wasn't exactly my forte when it came to natural talents anyway. It was only an 8- or 9-week class before I moved on to computers or something else that would occupy my time so I would just make my way through it. However, it's a story my mom and I still share often, and every single time, that same sinking feeling in my stomach comes back. I see middle school me feeling alone and scared in a room full of my peers, wanting to disappear into thin air. It was the first time I felt ashamed of having Tourette Syndrome. Sometimes I wonder what would have happened if I said something to him, would he have believed me? Would he have apologized? I guess it's something that I'll never know the answer to and maybe it's my fault, but nonetheless, it's a moment I'll take with me forever.

Although that memory made me feel timid and nervous about bringing my disorder up to teachers moving forward, I didn't let it stop me. I had a mission and I wasn't going to stop until everyone I knew and then some, knew about this disorder and what it really was. With that being said, flash-forward to my sophomore year in high school sitting in one of my favorite teacher's English classes. On Fridays, he would have time for us to write in journals for the whole period that only he would read unless we chose to share them with the class or a neighbor. This was a day where he allowed us to write about anything we wanted to tell him so of course, I decided to take the time to tell him about Tourette Syndrome. I remember opening up my red folder staring at the paper in front of me, when I decided to write about the day that I knew something was different, about the time where my body consciously made it known that my body no longer belonged to me—giving as much detail as I could within the time limit we were given. I remember writing up until the last few minutes of class, getting up to turn it in right before the bell rang, being excited and anxious to see what he was going to say about my story after he read it.

I don't remember a lot about anything he said in particular. I remember seeing the red marks on my journal and him thanking me for sharing such an intimate time in my life. But, what my mother and I remember most is what came after that day. My mom received a letter in the mail about a parent-teacher conference for that class. I was always a good student and rarely had to have my parents come in for conferences so we were both confused and, in all honesty, I'm pretty sure my mom thought about not even going to it. She knew I was doing well in the class so she didn't understand what this teacher wanted to speak to her about, but she went anyway. The day came where she went in to talk to my teacher and that is when she found out that Mr. S only asked her to come in so he could learn more about my disorder. He wanted to know that he was doing everything he could to make my learning environment a safe and happy one. He didn't know a lot about my disorder like most of my teachers before and after him, and he wanted to make sure he changed that. It was such a simple act, a simple gesture, but it meant so much to both of us. That wasn't the only reason he was one of my favorite teachers, but it certainly helped. He might not remember doing that, but I will never forget it.

These stories are important to share with everyone because they were two defining moments for me in school. That moment in middle school could have stopped me from sharing my story ever again. It could have shut me down, never feeling safe to share my true self again, but something told me not to let that moment stop me. I knew more people needed to know about this disorder,;I knew that there were kids everywhere experiencing those moments daily while getting kicked out of classrooms because teachers didn't believe them. I was fighting for something bigger than myself and I think a part of me knew that even at a young age.

When that moment came sophomore year when Mr. S showed me what it meant to be a caring teacher, he helped prove to me that being honest with myself and those around me was the right decision. He showed me that people care and how such a small, tiny gesture can be a moment that will stay with not only me but my mother forever. If there are teachers out there reading this, I beg you, do not give up on those difficult students. I know it's not easy and you're going to want to give up, but remember that for that student, you may be all they have to succeed. Remember that one sentence and one look can stay with a student for the rest of their lives, so always make it a good one. You never know what kind of battles your students are facing that you can't always see.

Teacher Reflection:

To the teachers reading this book, take this time to reflect on how you can make your classroom an inclusive environment. Do your students feel safe, included, and like they can thrive in the environment around them?

What am I doing right now to ensure all students are included?

_____

_____

_____

_____

What can I do to better understand and get to know my students on a deeper level?

_____

_____

_____

_____

Are any of my students struggling silently? How can I find out or help?

_____

_____

_____

_____

What can I change right now to ensure my students are getting the best out of the classroom?

_____

_____

_____

_____

What type of check-ins will provide the most productivity for both me and my students (weekly, bi-weekly, monthly, etc.)?

_____

_____

_____

_____

What small act of kindness can I perform to begin to build my students' trust in and outside of the classroom?

_____

_____

_____

_____

Is what I am doing right now going to make an impact on my students' lives?

_____

_____

_____

_____

Do I make any snap judgments about students with disabilities in my classroom

without meaning to do so? How can I do better to ensure this doesn't happen?

_____

_____

_____

_____

How can I best support all my students that walk into my classroom?

_____

_____

_____

_____

CHAPTER 9

My Struggle with Accepting Medication

Taking a pill to feel normal is one of the hardest decisions I had to come to terms with throughout this journey. I always prided myself on my strength, resilience, and having a positive attitude when it came to my disorder. When it comes to my mild case, most of the time I have been able to figure out my non-medical way to cope with my body moving uncontrollably. My mom and I both agreed at a young age that that little orange bottle was something that I didn't need. But, then my senior year of high school rolled around and my tics sort of took over my life.

There was so much going on in my life—good and bad, it was hard to face it all on my own. Emotions of any kind tend to exacerbate tics for a lot of people and for me, stress and excitement have always been my biggest contributing factors to bad tic days. I was worried about college coming up, what to major in, which school to go to, and my consideration to take a year off before I started. I was finishing what I thought was my last year of dance, which brought an overwhelming amount of emotions as dance was my one safe place from the tics. Because of all of this, my Tourettes fed off of the increased stress I had throughout the year. It wasn't until I found myself crying in my mom's lap almost every night for a few weeks straight that I finally realized that medication was my only option. I remember walking out to the backyard, looking for her for comfort after another terrible day, when I looked up at her with tears in my eyes and said, "I think I need to look at my options for medication." She didn't even have to say anything; we both knew I had to at least try.

My mom never thought medication was necessary and I can't blame her for coming to that conclusion. When I was seven, my only options were to take a pill in hopes that it would decrease my tics, but then I would have to take another one, just to offset some of the side effects from the first. It was going to be a terrible domino effect and my mother did not want me to have to go through that if it wasn't necessary. I was a child and she didn't want to see me go through even more on top of what the tics would already do to me. But, as I got older she let me make that decision because it was ultimately up to me and I knew my body best. We talked about it and she gave me her input, but ultimately the decision was up to me. It was my life and only I knew how bad things were mentally and physically.

I didn't struggle with this decision because I see nothing wrong with medication or anything of that sort. It has helped so many people in so many different ways and it's amazing what science has done. But for me, taking a pill meant I was giving up. I would often think to myself, "If I need help, then that means I'm not as strong as I constantly tell myself I am." I beat myself up about the decision even though deep down I knew it was what I needed to do if I wanted to have any kind of resemblance of a life. So, I made the appointment and waited through the fight with my mind mentally for four months before I finally got in to see my neurologist. I worked on breathing exercises with my mom, practiced my dances a lot, and did everything I could to keep my mind concentrated on anything other than the tics until I was able to get some medicated help. Looking back, I shake my head at those thoughts and doubts, because in reality, it took more strength to overcome those fears and make that decision for myself.

I was on a medication called Topamax throughout my entire senior year of high school. It's important to keep in mind that there is no cure for Tourette Syndrome, so my tics did not disappear completely, but the medicine was a huge help and gave me the break that I was hoping for but at a cost. The side effects were awful, especially in the beginning. I was taking nausea medicine daily to combat the constant stomach aches that I faced while my body adjusted. Additionally, I would get a tingly/prickly feeling throughout my fingers and my toes. You know how when your hands and feet fall asleep and when they "wake back up" it feels like being poked by thousands of tiny little needles? It doesn't necessarily hurt, but it's super uncomfortable. That's how it would feel during random parts of my day. I never knew when it was going to happen, but there was never a day where it didn't happen.

After the excitement from my senior year died down, I weaned off my medication and was pill-free for about a year. After a lot of consideration, I decided to take a year off school before I started college. I have always been the type to get stressed out easily, and after everything my body went through, it seemed like the right choice for me. I naively thought that I was going to get lucky and make it through my college career without having to turn back to my medication. Ultimately, working full-time while going to school full-time caught up to me and my tics were at an all-time high. I was ticcing constantly because there was always something for me to be stressed and worried about. I was balancing what most college students do with the added weight of Tourette Syndrome, so the time came where I had to make a tough decision yet again. I talked to my mom about it again and my boyfriend at the time (now husband), listening to their opinions and taking to heart everything they had to say. They didn't want to tell me what to do because they knew how hard it was for me to accept, but thankfully let me vent and cry to them when the decision was too much for me to think about. And after my now husband proposed to me and I added planning a wedding, moving out, and buying a home into the mix, I knew I had no other option.

Some people don't always realize what physical and emotional pain a person can go through while living with TS. Having no control over what my body is doing is hard to cope with, especially on the days where it feels like my body is never going to give me a break. There have been tears shed, muscle aches, headaches, stomach aches, and many more over the years with this disorder. As I grew into adulthood and started to have more stressors and excitement in my life, my tics began to increase. I remember getting so angry about it because all my life I have been told that they would get better as I got older and it seemed like it was the complete opposite for me. "Why couldn't they go away like I was told they were going to do?" I was getting worse as I was getting older and I just kept thinking, "This isn't fair; this was when I was supposed to get my body back." So, it made it that much harder for me to admit yet again, that I needed help.

I was on medication throughout the rest of my college career and when I think back on it, I don't think I would have been able to cope without it. I had so many things going on in my life that there was never a day where my tics didn't make themselves known. I had so many life-changing things happening at once, so the excitement kept building, and not using medication just wasn't an option at that point. It took a long time to realize that taking a pill didn't take away from the strength I liked to think I had but made me that much stronger to admit I couldn't do it alone anymore. Actually, in retrospect, that was probably one of my strongest moments when it came to my disorder. I had to put my pride aside and admit something I never wanted to admit—that I couldn't do it on my own and that was okay.

For me, my disorder is both my biggest weakness and my biggest strength. No parent or child wants to be on medication, but when it's starting to become both emotionally and physically draining, you're often left with no other choice. I encourage everyone to look at all their options and find something that gives them relief in their lives. I know now that it doesn't mean you're giving up, or that you're weak; it means you're strong enough to admit that you need help. There are so many other medications out there that treat and help disorders that interfere with day-to-day life and no one bats an eye when it comes to taking those. But when it comes to mental health or even Tourette Syndrome, this stigma seems to come with it. This stigma of needing a pill to get through my day weighed heavily on my mind and it's what made me so hesitant to admit I needed it. But, it's perfectly okay that I did. Someone once told me that you wouldn't expect a mechanic to work without any tools, and taking medication to get by is the same thing. It was such a simple comparison, but it was like a lightbulb going off in my head. We all have our struggles and we all need the right tools to get the job done.

CHAPTER 10

My Escape

A lthough my friends and family have always been there and comforted me on the worst of days, there was always that want to escape into something else. Unfortunately, when someone is on the other side of this disorder, there is only so much that they can do to help us, and until someone somewhere can find a way to make it go away for good, we have to find other ways to make our way through this crazy disorder. A lot of us have our hobbies or interests that bring our minds into a different and more comfortable world and for me, that world was dance. The dance studio, the stage, the music—they were everything to me for such a huge part of my life and it's something I'll always be grateful to have had.

My mom put me in dance class when I was just three years old. My older cousin danced, so she thought it could be something fun for me to try, not knowing then what a passion and deep-rooted love would blossom from it. In the beginning, it was my basic classes where I would get to shuffle and stomp my feet in tap shoes with giant black bows on them, wear tutus, and spin around not knowing which way to go or how to balance myself at the time. That grew into bigger tap shoes without bows, the tutus were no longer a part of my wardrobe, and I like to think I began to have much better dance moves, lifelong friends, and most importantly, an escape from every bad thing that ever happened to me, most importantly my tics.

My mom told me that she had to bribe me to get on stage during my first dance recital. Apparently, there was a part of the dance where a boy was going to have to spin me around in a circle and I wanted no part in it on the stage. So, my mom made a deal with me—I go on the stage and dance, and afterward, I get ice cream. (To this day I still blame her for my "addiction" to ice cream.) But, the deal worked and on the stage, I went. I danced to "Do You Believe in Magic" by The Lovin' Spoonful and wore a pink dress that had oversized ruffles on the sleeves and at the bottom. We toe-heeled and stomped all over the stage while people cheered and laughed at our inability to correctly dance to the music. Ever since that moment I was hooked.

As I got older and my love of dance grew, I began to love it for more than the rush of the stage and the cheering audience. Once I got old enough to know my body better and realized that having control over it wasn't always an option for me, dance became everything to me. Having control over your own body is something that a lot of people don't realize they are taking for granted every single day. It makes a lot of sense of course, because why would they? Moving our bodies is something that is second nature to most people; it's just what we're supposed to be able to do on our own terms. But for people like me who have Tourette Syndrome, that's a luxury we know nothing about. I was too young to remember a time *before* the tics. But, luckily, I remember all the times in dance when they disappeared.

The dance studio was a place where I existed in the moment. It was a place where I didn't have to worry about what my body was going to do next because for once in my life, I was in control. If I kicked my leg up in the air, threw my hands, or jumped and spun around, I did it because it was a part of the choreography. It was overwhelmingly perfect and the best part of all my days. I used to count down the hours on a bad tic day, knowing that all I had to do was make it to that studio, hear that music, and release. So many emotions ran through my body every time I danced that most people knew nothing about.

As corny as it sounds, I felt like I was home when I danced. Although the dances got harder, my determination grew with each year. I knew I wasn't the best dancer to ever grace the stage, but I knew there was something inside of me that was bursting to get out—and for the first time, it wasn't my tics desperate to escape me. I'm not sure how it happened, but somehow, I was just a normal kid when I entered the studio. The harder I danced, the further away Tourette Syndrome went, so much so that there were times when I forgot it even existed. I was in my own little world of normalcy and I never wanted it to end.

I practiced constantly. When I was in my younger years of dance, the practice didn't come as easily to me, and my mother had to push me to do it. But as I got older, I saw the beauty and the necessity in it. I always needed to perfect everything,especially my dances. I wanted my teachers to notice how hard I worked in and outside of the dance studio. I wanted to stand out for something that wasn't awkward body movements or noises. I wanted to stand out for something good and to make my parents and my teachers proud of me. I loved dancing and I loved knowing that I was in control. So, I practiced making sure I could get it as perfect as possible. It was a blessing and a curse since that perfectionist in me led me to be incredibly hard on myself any time I messed up on stage. The rest of the dance could have been perfect and one wrong turn, one count off, and I would be thinking about it the rest of the day. I would beat myself up over it because, in my mind and the dance world, everything had to be perfect when it came time for the stage.

The blessings of my dance life heavily outweighed any negatives that came with it. The perfectionism, the pounds of makeup, the itchy uncomfortable dance costumes, the cuts, bruises, and pulled muscles— every ounce of it was worth it to me. The world of dance brought something into my life that I will never get anywhere else. Other athletic activities come close; exercising always helps on a bad day, or focusing my mind on other hobbies and interests, but none of them come close to the escape I felt while dancing. It was something that I will sadly not get back, but I'm thankful for every moment I had with it.

I danced for 20 years throughout my life. I started when I was three and took a small break after I turned 18 since my studio no longer offered classes for students after high school. A few years later I found a studio that offered classes for adults, where we got to perform in the recital, and just like that my love was back. I decided that I wanted to hit 20 years before I stopped for good. My love never faded, and the studio and the stage still provided the same escape that I came accustomed to when I was younger, but my body just couldn't handle it anymore. So, I decided I would end my last year with a solo that was inspired by my life with Tourette Syndrome.

Ending that part of my life wasn't an easy decision and it's still emotional for me to think about at times. But, ending it with a dance inspired by the one thing that it took away from me only made sense. I danced to Kelly Clarkson's song— "Invincible." The song always spoke to me on a deeper level because of my disorder, and it meant a lot to me because of that. I had a few that I relate to that part of my life, but my teacher and I thought that one made the most sense for what I wanted to accomplish with the piece. My costume was a black and teal color, with a flowing skirt that floated through the air when- ever I kicked, jumped, or turned. It was a contemporary piece, and the first one I ever did in my dancing career, and the one dance that meant the most to me. It was another way for me to share my story, while also, sadly saying goodbye to another.

I'm not the only one who has experienced these "breaks" from

Tourette Syndrome due to exercise or an activity of some kind. A lot of people have asked me what has helped tic reduction outside of medication. Although I always preface this with telling everyone I'm not a doctor and this is what helps *me*, I cannot say enough about doing something active. Over the years, research has also shown the benefits from physical activity and the decrease in tics. A study performed in 2020 showed a group of people who lived with Tourette Syndrome showed a decrease in tics during and after kickboxing. Because of this, it is said that physical exercise can play a huge part in lessening the severity of tics at least for a short period of time (Jackson et al.2020).

Knowing that studies are being done and they are showing to be helpful only makes me recommend that type of relief more. I want everyone to have that break, to have those moments in their lives when they can get control back, even if for just an hour or so. I think there is also something to be said about how the same effects could come from gym class in school. It's that one time throughout the day where kids can let out the pent-up energy they have been holding in all day long. Gaining that composure can be such a powerful tool for a person or child with Tourette Syndrome; it's all a matter of finding what that escape is for everyone.

Although I do feel that gym class helped as well as other after-school programs, dance was always the constant that brought my body back. It wasn't just an extracurricular activity for me. Dance was my whole world for so long and saying goodbye to that part of my life and to that escape from every "bad" part of me is something I will always miss. But, I'm so thankful for every moment of it. My mother didn't know it at the time, but her bringing me to my first dance class was the best gift she's ever given me.

CHAPTER 11

My Support System

Growing up with Tourette Syndrome hasn't always been easy. Despite my positivity and my drive to never let it beat me, some days ended in resentment, exhaustion, and tears. I would be exhausted from the non-stop movement that my body/brain forced upon me, angry and upset because of how badly I wanted the control back, and angry because in my head I was letting it win. I've always had that mantra—"Never Let Tourette Syndrome Win." I think it carried me through most of my life and I've always stuck strongly by that. But on those bad days, that mantra of mine sometimes did more harm than good. I felt like I was letting myself down. It's been a mental battle for me ever since I can remember. When another bad day comes, I know those thoughts and negative feelings will return and it will always be a never-ending cycle. This is where I would turn to my family and friends for support. When my mind and body weren't my own anymore, I needed someone to bring me back down to earth and remind me to do one simple thing—BREATHE.

I grew up with a fairly large and loving extended family. I only had one older brother who always had my back, especially when it came to this disorder, and my mom and dad were and have been together my whole life. But the larger part came with aunts, uncles, and 20+ cousins who were my best friends and basically additional siblings while growing up. Obviously, we told the whole family about my condition when I was diagnosed, and I never remember anyone ever making it seem like it was a big deal. I didn't see the sadness in their eyes or worry for my future. I'm positive it was there, but never in front of me. It's like they instinctively knew what I needed from them, and I am eternally grateful for that. Being around my family was a safe place to tic no matter how big or small they were and believe me when I was a child, my tics were much bigger and complex. But, even with all that, they never made me feel alone or like I was burdening them with anything I was doing. I would get the occasional curious question "what are you doing" if it was a tic they've never seen before, or they would ask if I was okay and that worked for me. They will never know how much their acceptance, love, and compassion for me growing up meant to me and how it helped mold my mindset into what it is today.

Although my family was huge, my real backbone through this whole thing was 100% my parents. I knew that without a doubt they would be there to catch me every time I would fall. My mom was my best friend growing up;she still is to this day, and now that I am an adult, I can look back and see just how much she did for me. She will know what kind of phone call it's going to be just by the way I say "Mom" or "Hi" when she picks up, and hearing her voice on the other end of the phone instantly comforts me every single time. She knew how to calm me down in just the right way. When a tic attack would happen, it didn't matter what she was doing, she would be beside me, rubbing my back or playing with my hair while helping me to focus on my breathing. "In through your nose and out through your mouth," she would tell me often, having to repeat herself while I would get worked up repeatedly.

My mom was always the perfect balance while I was growing up. She was my mom when she needed to be a mom, and more importantly, she was my friend when I needed a friend. She never made me feel bad for who I was and never made a big deal of it either. She knew I had something that could make life hard, but she never told me that. She helped me to learn what I could do, instead of the things I couldn't. Whenever I told her how much I hated having this disorder, whenever I cried, she didn't make me feel like my sadness didn't matter. She didn't tell me that other people had bigger problems or that I was lucky because I had a mild case. She just let me feel what I needed to feel in those moments. I don't think she realizes how those small moments meant everything to me. I was her daughter, and the pain I was feeling was real, even if she didn't understand it firsthand, and I think that is so incredibly important. I don't know how to explain it, but she just knew. She was meant to be a mother of a child with Tourette Syndrome because she was and still is caring, selfless, and a calming force to be around.

My dad, on the other hand, had a different coping mechanism when it came to my Tourette Syndrome. He hated to see me tic and he still does. I don't remember him showing that when I was a child, or maybe I was just too naïve to see it on his face, but now that I'm an adult, I can see how it hurts him to know that he can't make it go away. His technique has and always will be laughter. You see, my dad *lives* to see the people he loves laugh and smile. He will go to great lengths just to hear us laugh—often at his own expense. He always does the same thing though; I can hear him in my head as I type this, "Brit, are you okay?" when I start to flick my head or roll my eyes constantly. Always, I nod and say, "Yea, I'm fine," because even when it won't stop, I know I am because he's right there. Usually a joke or something ridiculous will come flying out of his mouth soon after, and looking back, I know he was doing that for me. He would take me out of that moment and bring me back to what was happening with his quick check-in and quick, sometimes incredibly corny, jokes. His jokes and words of encouragement will always mean the most to me.

My dad was never the type of person to verbally say the things he felt in his heart—he still isn't. But, he had a way with words when he could write or type them out when he needed to. My mom always jokes and says that I am the female version of him and I can't disagree. There are so many things I get from my father and I know because of that, he blames himself for what some people would call my "problems." But what he doesn't know is that I'm so proud to be a little version of him. He gave me my strength to never back down, he made me feel empowered to never, ever, let someone take advantage of me or make jokes at my expense when it came to my disorder. Without him, I wouldn't be half as strong as I am today.

I wish I could sit here and give you a run-down of every single person in my family, but I don't think anyone has that kind of time. So instead, I'll do my best to sum up how incredible my family was.... I could sum it up by just telling you that I was one of the lucky ones. Like I said earlier, it was as if everyone instinctively knew what to do. They might feel differently, but that's how I see it. They showed how much they cared about me by just letting me be myself. It's as simple as that. They knew the tics could come at any point. I could be laughing and having a great time one minute and I could go into a tic attack the next. It didn't happen often as I was outside playing with my brother and my cousins, but when it did, they would sit with me, make sure I was okay, and go to get my mom if needed.

I remember one time, in particular, my husband and I were out of town visiting my brother and we were out with his friends when I felt my stomach start to contract in and out aggressively. I felt my breath getting shorter and felt the panic of being in a public place start to set in. I was suddenly very aware that I was around people that might not have known I had Tourette Syndrome. I felt my head start to tilt back and I tried with all my might to keep it forward. I was trying to suppress it as best I could and hope that no one would notice the weird girl who couldn't sit still. I tried to keep it under control because

I didn't want to ruin anyone's night, but my brother looked over at me and immediately knew I needed to leave. He didn't hesitate for a second; he didn't care that he had to leave his friends or that I ended the night early. I don't know if he remembers that, but I do, and that small moment is something I don't know if I will ever forget. He's not always great with expressing his feelings either, but it's in those small moments that I know he will always have my back.

I'm blessed because my life is filled with moments like the ones I spoke about. But, not everyone is as fortunate to have a supporting family. It breaks my heart every time I see it, but there are just some people out there that don't have the compassion that is needed to be a parent, family member, or even a friend of someone with Tourette Syndrome. I know it can be annoying to the people around us; everyone who tics knows that, and I can almost guarantee that it is not something that runs through all of our minds while we tic in public. You never know who is going to say something or make a big deal about it and that can be terrifying. That is why I am grateful to every single person in my life who has let me be me around them and for every family function where I could tic as much as I want and know that no one would or will ever say anything about it. My hope to the person reading this who has a child or knows someone with Tourette Syndrome is for them to be that person for someone else. I may have had an army of support while growing up, but not everyone does. Try to be that advocate, that person they feel comfortable around, and let them know that they have support in you. It can make the world of difference in the life of someone with Tourette Syndrome or any other disorder or disability.

Support System Reflection:

For those reading this book that know someone with Tourette Syndrome or something similar such as anxiety, OCD, ADD, ADHD, etc., use these reflection pages to help you work through how you can support, love, and help those people in your life in the way that they need.

How am I supporting those I love with Tourette Syndrome or a similar

experience right now?

_____

_____

_____

_____

What can I do to let my loved one, friend, co-worker, know that I am here for

them?

_____

_____

_____

_____

Do I create an environment at home, work, or school where the people I care about can be open and honest with me?

_____

_____

_____

_____

What is one small thing I can do to help the person I am supporting through Tourette Syndrome or something similar? Talking, small signals, etc.?

_____

_____

_____

_____

Sometimes it can be hard to see past the tics, so what am I doing to better understand and accept my child, friend, student?

_____

_____

_____

_____

CHAPTER 12

Love and The Fears That Come with It

F inding friends who knew how to accept me and handle me at my worst was a struggle in itself, let alone finding a boy or a man who I thought would stick around through all that Tourette Syndrome had to offer. Throughout middle school and high school, I had the usual crushes and "boyfriends" that wrote me a note every once in a while, and maybe we'd even hold hands in the hallway before class. But, I never really had any real boyfriends until after I graduated high school. Telling the boys that I dated about Tourette Syndrome was my way of weeding out all the bad ones. There were still a couple that slipped through the cracks, but for the most part, that's what showed me if they were worth my time. Being the honest person that I am, Tourette Syndrome was one of the first things that would come up, and the boy's reaction would be what I would judge them on. Maybe some see that as a bad thing, but for me, I didn't want to waste my time or fall for someone that wasn't going to be there for me in the end.

Before I met my husband, Scott, I was scared I would never find someone who could really love me. I used to think, "Maybe it's not in the cards for me, that future with someone who would love every bit of me." The me that I would rather keep hidden, but have no choice but to share with the world. I used to think to myself that finding someone who would accept every little movement, every quirk, and every pain that came with Tourette Syndrome would be impossible. "If I annoy myself half the time, how could I ever expect someone else to not feel the same way?"

I'm not saying these thoughts I used to have were something I thought about all the time. I never voiced those fears to anyone while growing up. I didn't want someone to sit and tell me how silly it was to think that or give me a list of reasons why I was wrong. I guess I just didn't think someone, even a family member who loved and cared about me, would understand my feelings. As much as they tried, no one truly knew what it was like for me and why I was so afraid of never finding what most girls grew up dreaming about having.

Through a few of the boys I dated, there were jokes made sometimes, nothing terrible by any means, but sometimes more than I was comfortable with. But, as strong as I like to think I am, I let some relationships go on for too long and by "too long" I mean only a couple of months. It wasn't until I met my husband, Scott, did I know what it meant to truly be loved for every single part of me. Scott seemed like he was too good to be true at first; sometimes it still feels like that because of how incredible he is. We took our time getting to know each other for a few months before we finally found the right time for us to start our relationship, but it worked out exactly how it should have.

Just as I did with anyone else, I told Scott about having Tourette Syndrome from the very beginning—the very first time we met to be exact. I remember almost everything from that night. From the butterflies in my stomach to hearing the gravel move in my parent's driveway when he pulled up in his black SRT-4 to pick me up for the evening. We thought we were going to Starbucks for an hour or so, only to find out that it was closed which led us to the restaurant Perkins across the street. That turned into four hours of getting to know each other while we talked about what seemed like everything and because of that, my life with Tourette Syndrome was brought up. I remember watching him as he legitimately listened to me explain what it was and how it affected my life. He even admitted that he had some ignorance towards the disorder in his younger years, which instead of making me negatively judge him, made me realize what an honest and open person he was willing to be with me. It can't always be easy telling a person with a disorder that you may have made a few jokes here and there in the past, and I respected that.

It might sound crazy but I knew pretty early on that he was something special that I had to hold on to. One evening I had him watch a movie called "Front of the Class," which is a Hallmark Channel Movie about an inspirational man named Brad Cohen, who also had Tourette Syndrome while growing up, and became a teacher and a vice-principal of a school. His story has always been a motivation in my life and he is someone who I have always looked up to. I had him watch this movie because I wanted him to see another side and face of Tourette Syndrome; I wanted Scott to know what this disorder was capable of doing to me sometimes because I knew I was falling fast, and I couldn't handle it going any further if he couldn't accept the biggest part of me.

After the movie ended, I was lying there next to him with a thousand thoughts going through my head while trying to hold back tears. *What if this is too much, what if he can't handle something like this? What if one day he becomes annoyed or frustrated with me never being able to sit still?* I kept thinking about situations like this in my head until I finally got the courage to just ask him.

"Are you sure this will never be too much for you?"

He looked at me as if I was a crazy person, shook his head at me like he often does, looked me straight in the eyes, and said, "I promise this will NEVER be too much for me. I love you because of who

Tourettes made you. It turned you into the strong girl that I fell in love with and that's not going to change."

I remember not having any words to say after that. All I could think about was how I didn't want that moment to end. There has never been a time in my life before that moment that made me feel so beautiful, strong, and loved *because* of my disorder and not despite it. It was at that moment that I knew without a doubt that he was going to be the man I would marry because I could see the passion in his eyes staring back at me, and that was a feeling I would never let go of.

I bring myself back to that moment often because it makes me smile and brings those butterflies back into my stomach in the best way possible. It's hard to believe that it's been 12 years with him by my side, but similar to when I said my mother was meant to love a child with Tourette Syndrome, my husband was meant to love a woman with it as well. His patience has always been something I admire and his selflessness is something I could never come close to. He has believed in every crazy endeavor I've ever had no matter how big and has helped me along the way. Because of him, I developed the courage to share my story with the world on social media. I began an awareness event every year and will continue to do so year after year. He loved me through something I thought no one ever would and I'm not sure how I was the one he chose to spend his life with. A lot of people with Tourette Syndrome feel as though no one will ever love them through it, and I was certainly one of those people, but I'm here to tell you that it's possible. You just have to be patient until that right person comes along and loves every piece of you.

CHAPTER 13
When the Support System Doesn't Show Up

W hile advocating and sharing my story about my family and what they have done for me, I have unfortunately come across so many people who do not have that family support. I'm told by people that they don't feel safe ticcing in front of their parents, that they are told to stop, or they don't believe them when they say they can't control it. Comments like these completely shatter my heart. I want everyone to feel loved, supported, and welcomed in their own home. But, I also know that in the world we live in, that's just simply not always the case.

The sad truth is even when a doctor is staring at a parent, telling them that their child has Tourette Syndrome, they still choose not to believe the movements, sounds, and noises they make aren't completely out of their control. In these instances, I don't have first-hand experience. I wish I could tell you all of these magnificent things to do if you're one of those people reading this book, but I'm not sure that I can. But, what I can offer is the love and support from not only me but an entire community online. This is where social media can be a really beautiful thing. It can be full of naysayers, "trolls,, and cruel people, but it can also be where someone can find their tribe or second family. It can be a safe place to vent to those that truly understand what someone is going through.

Sometimes the most powerful words someone can hear are "I do that too" or "I completely understand." When I first started doing advocacy videos and bringing others with Tourette Syndrome onto them on YouTube, I didn't realize how much I needed to hear those words too or what a difference it made. I can pause in the middle of my sentences because it's hard to tic while talking and the person on camera understands how completely normal it is for us. I don't feel bad when I can't answer right away or a tic interrupts something we are trying to discuss. They are ticcing right along with me and it's as if nothing odd or weird is happening at all. I cannot explain what a freeing experience that can be, especially if that's not felt within a home.

It sounds silly, but a quick video chat, direct message, or IM conversation can be just what someone needs that isn't used to feeling loved and supported for something they cannot help. It can provide that safe place where someone can finally tic freely without being yelled at or told to stop. It can be a place to vent with someone who understands. Most importantly, it can become a place where a child or an adult doesn't feel so alone and misunderstood. Loneliness often accompanies those with Tourette Syndrome and finding that family online can be scary, but so worth it.

CHAPTER 14

From a Family's Perspective

F rom *Britney's Mother:*
How do you tell a seven-year-old the reason she can't control her own body? How do you tell her that there is no cure and that there is no medicine that can really help?

When Britney was diagnosed, these were the questions I asked myself. The internet was new, so anything I got about Tourettes was mostly clinical. Nothing personal to help me understand what she was experiencing, or what I could do to help her. So as a family we learned together.

We never wanted Britney to feel like something was wrong. We wanted her to feel like Tourettes was not a bad thing. Although some days it was a bad thing. On those days we had to figure out what would work best to help. I would find something to redirect her mind, like a puzzle or a word search. If that didn't work, we would have her do breathing exercises. When that didn't work, unfortunately she just had to let the tic attack play out. Those were and are the days that break my heart. As her mom it's my job to ease her pain. So what do you do when you can't help?

With everything Britney has gone through with her Tourette

Syndrome, she never let it beat her. She took her diagnosis and turned it into advocacy. We are very proud of her and everything that she has accomplished.

From Britney's Father:

How I felt when Britney was first diagnosed with Tourettes...where do I start? I'll start by saying I was scared for Britney's wellbeing. She was just a little girl and none of us knew anything about what she was going through. I didn't know what to expect or how to handle it and I didn't want to let her see my concerns. I didn't want her to feel like she was different. I wanted her to know that she could accomplish anything she put her mind to and that she was just as capable as all the kids around her.

She has taken Tourette Syndrome head on, like it wasn't even a challenge for her even though I know it has been. Britney has worked so hard to spread awareness for Tourettes, to erase the stigma, to educate people that it's not just a joke like the movies display, it's not just a punchline.

To be honest, I have always felt helpless. There isn't much I can do to help her and that kills me. We were recently on a family vacation where I saw her ticcing a lot that week. It hurts me to see it and I know it's even worse for her. I just wish I could do something more.

From Britney's Husband:

We were only a few hours into our very first date when Britney did a brave thing and told me she had Tourette's. Over the last 12 years I have since seen her become even more brave as she shares her story to educate and help thousands of people. It wasn't always easy for her, and I have witnessed the good and bad days along the way.

For anyone that is getting to know someone with Tourette's or maybe even starting to date someone with it or something similar, my biggest advice is to have empathy. Try your best to put yourself in their shoes and truly try to understand what they are going through. I will admit I was a little taken back by her telling me on our first date, and I really didn't know anything about Tourette Syndrome, but I think it was the best thing she could have done. She has absolutely made me a more patient, understanding person, and her telling me that right away allowed her to learn if I was going to be a good person for her.

I try to be the best partner I can be. On her bad days, I do whatever little things I can to make them better. I can't make Tourette's go away unfortunately. I can't make her tics stop. But I can rub her back and shoulders. I can stop and comfort her. I can give her more time to do things and not make a big deal about it. I can take other things off her plate that day so she has less to stress about. It's always about the little things, and it's important to me that I never forget that. Writing this book is literally Britney's biggest dream come true, and I never had a doubt that she would make it happen. I have seen her story have such a positive impact already, and I know she isn't even close to finished.

CHAPTER 15

Working with a Disability

Disability... that word is a difficult one for me to accept and always has been. I hate referring to Tourette Syndrome as a disability, but at the end of the day, that's exactly what it is. I think my struggle to accept the word stems from never wanting anyone to look at me with pity or treat me any differently, especially when it comes to my working career. The public often sees or hears the word disability and instantly thinks of something awful. I think knowing that and having that mentality all around me is what made me so hesitant for so long to come to terms with my life as a disabled person. This also made it difficult for me to be vulnerable and honest while entering the work-force. I've constantly gone back and forth, wondering before, during, and after all my interviews if bringing up Tourette Syndrome would hinder my chances at getting the job or progressing at a job. You never know what people are thinking during an interview, especially if you bring up something like Tourette Syndrome.

Although I constantly worry and wonder if I make the right choice in the interview and hiring process, I ultimately always decide to bring up my disorder during my interview when I can. At the end of the day, if they're hiring me, then they need to hire every part that comes with me. There's no chance of me progressing and creating a career at a business if I can't feel comfortable being myself, tics and all. I'm not saying it's easy to feel comfortable ticcing in front of my coworkers, because it never is and never will be. But, if I had to tic while at work around a bunch of people who didn't know what I was doing and most likely making all sorts of crazy assumptions about me, it would be that much worse and cause some very bad after-work nights for me. That is something that I just never wanted to deal with, nor do I anytime soon.

There has only been one job where I didn't get the chance to bring up my situation in my interview. There just wasn't an opening for me to discuss it and I always wanted it to come out naturally. I figured the more natural I sounded talking about it, the more natural they would receive it. Did that work in the interviews? I guess I wouldn't be able to tell you for sure or not, but it made sense to me so I rolled with it. At this time though, it was so hard for me to find my way to bring it into the conversation,which led to me having more anxiety about my tics in front of everyone. There was never an easy way to bring it up to coworkers, but I always felt it to be easier if management was aware of my disorder. It made me feel as though they "had my back" if and when it would ever come up. I'm sure there were times where this wasn't true and it's just what my mind made up to make me feel better, but either way, it worked for me and we have to do whatever works, right?

I don't know if I can remember exactly how I was able to bring it up after this, but I found my way through it. I found my openings through talking about doctor appointments, or if others talked about medical issues or problems, I tried to find a way to bring it up and what that taught me was that there are more good people out there than bad. Nine times out of 10, people just asked questions because they were genuinely curious and wanted to know more about me and Tourette Syndrome in general. Being open and honest with the people I spent the most time with made my time at work more enjoyable, and I felt like I could do whatever I needed to do, whenever I needed to do it to make things easier. I no longer felt the added stress of wondering what everyone around me thought about the weird movements or sounds I made at my desk or when I walked around.

I started out as an administrative assistant, where I moved into a Lease Accountant Role. It wasn't my dream job by any means, but I challenged myself with it and took on as much responsibility as I could. I was on a computer for eight hours a day, which caused me to tic incessantly with my mouse. I would constantly click and slam my mouse against my keyboard. I did this so much that as time went on, there were tiny chunks of the edge of my keyboard missing. I would stare at my keyboard sometimes wondering why I just couldn't control myself like everyone else. Every time I did it in that quiet office, it felt like the sound just echoed through the airways. To combat this feeling I would listen to music or podcasts so even I didn't have to hear the sounds like that I was making. No one ever made me feel like I was the burden my mind always told me I was and they often told me they never even noticed it, which I'm not sure I believed. But, either way, they were always accepting of me and the tics they were forced to listen to all day long.

This job reminded me how good people can be and the benefits of allowing myself to be vulnerable. Being honest with myself gave me the courage to ask our company to do a "Teal Day [Teal is the Tourette Awareness color in the U.S.]" at work to bring awareness for the disorder. Not only did they do the "Teal Day," but they surprised me with shirts of support that said, "For Britney" on them and made a whole day of it. It felt incredible and when I walked down to take our "Teal Day" photo and saw them all standing there with smiles on their faces, wearing their shirts and showing more support than they even realized, tears filled my eyes. I never worked with people who were so supportive, and I never would have experienced that moment had I not pushed down my fears of awkwardness or embarrassment and let them all into my life.

I've had more moments of good than bad when it comes to being honest about my disorder in the workplace, but it hasn't always been a bed of roses for me either. I've encountered some incredibly rude people who have said things to me that have stuck with me for years. While I want to tell this story, I want to make it clear, although the words this woman said to me have stuck with me for some time, I still do not regret being 100% honest with all of my coworkers. Sometimes the world shows the good with the bad and ugly things are said, but without times like those, I might not be able to really appreciate being around the good ones and I truly believe that wholeheartedly. Sometimes, I think people don't always understand what is outside of their realm, and I think that is what led to the interaction I had with a former coworker.

I worked in a very small office at this job, so small that I was told that before I started, it used to be a supply closet. We had five people shoved into it, so tempers could get hot from time to time. On this particular occasion though, everyone was getting along just fine. Tourette Syndrome happened to come up and I was answering some questions for a friend of mine— telling her what it was like for me, how I try to spread as much awareness and education as I possibly could because of the misconceptions and everything in between. I was getting into some of my stories about how there needs to be more awareness when a woman decided to uninvitingly join our conversation by saying, "Tourette Syndrome doesn't need or deserve as much awareness though, because people know what that is, and it's not as bad as like depression, or things like that." I was in total shock. I instantly felt my blood start to boil, my hands started to shake, and heat spread throughout my entire body. For being someone that never backs down from saying something back to someone, I was in such a state of total disbelief that I didn't even have the words to respond.

Even while writing this, I feel the intensity of anger and indignation that I felt at that moment.

I will never forget those words being spoken to me, or the look on her face and the nonchalant tone she had as if what she said wasn't incredibly hurtful and demeaning. I knew at that moment, if I didn't react carefully, that the words I used wouldn't have helped the situation and knowing me, could have gotten *me* fired for something *she* said. I can be a very temperamental person, especially when I feel insulted or attacked, so I knew I had to be cautious. I remember being quiet for a moment, as I turned around to face my computer when I said, "I don't think that's necessarily true. I don't compare disorders, but I can promise you that people don't 'know' about Tourette Syndrome, at least not enough." I'm pretty sure she said something else after that, but I was done listening. I wasn't going to argue over who has it worse, because I would never compare my situation to someone else's. I don't ever think that I have it so much worse than anyone else. Everyone is battling something that I would never be able to imagine, and because of that, it's not my place to compare or pass judgment.

After that day, I lost any respect I had for her. I just didn't and still don't know how someone can look at someone and tell them that their disorder that they've struggled with their entire lives didn't matter. It made me feel like everything I set out to do was being laughed at and that no one truly cared or understood. I remember questioning myself and the positive attitude I constantly tried to have when it came to my tics. *Was it giving off the wrong impression? Do they think I'm faking this?* Those words led me into some of the hardest few weeks I've ever had at work with my disorder. For a moment, I went into a dark place, not knowing if what I was doing was helping, not knowing if people just thought that because I didn't always tic at work that it would have to mean that it wasn't that bad. The anxiety of those thoughts made my tics run wild. I was crying almost every day at home and at work. I had to go to the restroom to gain my composure only to enter into the same room where I felt defeated and disrespected.

After a long talk with my husband, he convinced me that I needed to report what was said to me. That as much as I didn't like to admit it, I had a disability, and someone was belittling it and making me feel as if I didn't matter—as if every sleepless night, every tear, and every fight against my body just didn't matter because to her "it wasn't that bad." I didn't think reporting it would do any good and I didn't want to cause more drama or discomfort in the office for any of my coworkers. But, I knew he was right, so I went to my boss and told him about the incident. He seemed as though he was sympathetic at the time of me reporting it, but I'm sad to say, it didn't appear that anything was ever done. I don't know what I expected from it really, but it was the day I knew I wasn't respected as an individual, much less a human being.

It's hard for me to look back at that time because it's difficult for me to see how one woman made such an impact on my life so negatively. I'm sometimes ashamed of myself for giving her that much space in my mind and my life. But I say this because someone reading this might not realize what they're saying is hurting someone. They might not think it's that bad or even harmful in any way, but it's so important to think before you speak. I know it's a cliché saying, but it's true. Words are powerful and they're the one thing you can never take back, so be careful with what you say because like I said before, everyone is fighting something. Just because someone in your life might not have Tourette Syndrome, but lives with a different disorder doesn't give you the right to compare lives. We all deal with it in our own way, and going to work day after day into a building where I felt disrespected was hard. It took everything out of me and I found myself getting in a worse mood the closer I got to work every single day.

This moment allowed me to understand why it was so important for me to accept the disability definition of what I had. Owning that helped me to focus on what I needed and what I deserved. Just as any other employee, I deserved respect from those around me, especially when it came to Tourette Syndrome. I also needed accommodations from time to time and if my job wasn't willing to give me that, then I needed to find somewhere else to work. So, after this experience, while explaining what Tourette Syndrome was, I also began to disclose what I could need from them. With supervisors or management, I've explained how sometimes I may just need to walk away for a minute, go to the bathroom, or take a couple laps, but I'll be back. I explained how if I had the ability to do what my body needed me to do, then I'd be able to do what I needed to do in my job too.

I'm happy to say that I left that job and found my "home" when it comes to working. I'm in an incredible place that values its employees and understands when I may need to take some time because of what my body does to me. I have quiet spaces I can go to when things start to ramp up, and I have a team that is in full support of me one way or another and again. I would have never known the capacity of these kind people had I not opened up and shared some of my story with them. Not every interaction is going to be pleasant, and there will be people who don't understand or frankly don't want to understand, but that's fine. I know my days of encountering rude people are far from over, however, it will never stop me from spreading awareness and doing everything in my power to make everyone see that we are so much more than a joke and to finally erase the stigma that comes with Tourette Syndrome.

What Can Employers Do to Support an Employee with Tourette Syndrome?

- Talk to your employees. One person with Tourette Syndrome is just one person. Every single case is different and every person is different and wants/needs different things.

- Ensure the employee feels comfortable before telling other co-workers about their disorder. It's theirs and, therefore, no one else's story to tell to anyone else. They might have felt comfortable or felt a need to let you as their employer know, but that does not mean they feel comfortable telling the entire office. It should and needs to be the employees choice.

- If and when that employee feels comfortable, let them teach the company about their disorder. It can be such an eye-opening experience for everyone involved and allow the employee to feel seen, which is incredibly important.

- Give them a quiet area in the office where they can go when situations get overwhelming or their tics ramp up. This can also be good for the entire office for those moments when an employee just needs a break.

- Know that everyday can be different. A person with Tourette Syndrome may not tic in the same way or even the same severity from day to day. Tics can change as frequently as hour to hour.

- Allow the person to tic freely without condescending looks or tones and **never** ask the person to stop ticcing.

- Most importantly, don't make judgements before you learn. The last thing a workplace wants to do is assume the person cannot do something because they have Tourette Syndrome. They will let you know what, if any, limitations that they may have.

CHAPTER 16

Finding Strength in my Weakness

P eople that are a part of the Tourette Syndrome community tend to ask me how I learned to become so open about something so personal. Unfortunately, that is one of the most difficult questions for me to answer. I don't know if I will ever be able to give a straightforward "this is how you learn to accept your diagnosis and life" kind of guide or answer. The truth is, it takes time and has taken me my whole life to get to where I am with it now. I don't discredit the fact of how blessed I was while growing up with my family though, because I know they had a lot to do with who I am today, if not everything to do with it. They believed in me when I didn't believe in myself and always made me feel like I was capable of anything despite what all the statistics said about a person like me.

I know people are reading this that do not have that support system within their own families and it truly breaks my heart. I believe that family doesn't always mean blood and if you can find that connection and that sense of acceptance somewhere else, then, by all means, run to it with open arms. However, finding those people is and was just half the battle for me. I couldn't rely on the people around me to make me feel comfortable in my skin. I couldn't ask them to bring confidence into my life. I had to find that within myself and it takes some time—it still does. It might appear as though this disorder never bothers me, but those that are close to me know that that's not true. I have a love-hate relationship with Tourette Syndrome and I am confident that will never change. I have good days and bad days just like everyone else would, but I focus hard on those good days.

Every bad day gave me more strength. In the moment and the heat of the tics, I might be seeing things a little differently, but after I make it through—and I always do—I look back on myself almost with a sense of pride. I tell myself that there is no one else in the world who could deal with this disorder except me and everyone else living with it. I have something that makes me so unique and powerful because I live in a sense of mystery and curiosity about what my body is going to do next. I realize that sentence makes the tics seem a bit more magical than they are, but nonetheless, it's accurate. It was Greta Thunberg who once said "...under the right circumstances—being different is a super power." I think that she was onto something when she said that. We all have our own strengths and superpowers; some just come in different packaging.

As I said, this isn't the easiest of views or approaches to have on my bad days and believe me, I've had plenty of them. But, it's something we need to remind ourselves of so often. Learning to live with this disorder isn't something that happens overnight; it isn't even something that I believe can ever 100% happen because it's so unpredictable. If you've gone your whole life telling yourself that you'll never be able to do it, then you'll never be able to do it. It takes work to rewire your brain and believe in everything that you are and everything you're capable of becoming. It's very similar to how I've navigated through this crazy life. It's been over 20 years since my diagnosis, and it has been a fight every single day to feel my body do weird things and feel the stares from strangers around me. That's where that re-wiring comes in and that's what I constantly fall back on.

The positive re-wiring wasn't the only thing I had to focus on either. Another huge factor I had to come to terms with was accepting the days where I felt weak. This has been and always will be my biggest internal battle. I do not like "giving in" and accepting defeat; I never have. But, it's something I had to come to terms with while living inside a body that never truly felt like my own. The days where the tics started as soon as I woke up and lasted until I closed my eyes were the days I felt like a hypocrite. I preach this positive attitude and I'll always stand by that; however, the tears find me when every single muscle in my body hurts and is drained. I learned that not accepting the bad days was just as toxic as constant negativity. I'm human and some days are just flat-out hard and that's okay. It's okay to not always be okay, to not always smile, and not always see the "lesson" at that moment in time. I'll always feel stronger days, weeks, or months later for it, but in those moments, I had to tell myself that "it's okay that this hurts." I had to teach myself how I was allowed to not like my tics and still believe in who they've made me become. Tourette Syndrome is *hard*, and I was allowed to admit that.

Through the positivity and even the negativity battling in my brain, I still always told myself that if someone couldn't handle me because of Tourette Syndrome, then they have the bigger problems in life and not me. No one will ever be a bigger critic than the voice in my head. However, the difference is, I have no control over what my body is doing, but they certainly have control over how they react to it, especially after finding out the truth behind the movements. I didn't have the time to try and make them react the way I wanted them to or hoped that they would. Sometimes words and reactions stung a little more than others, but I had to find my way through it and figure out how to move on from it. Every time one of those comments was made only proved to me why it was so important to spread awareness and the truth about this disorder.

So, maybe it's not easy and maybe it has taken me 20 plus years to get to where I'm at now, but I believe that every little moment, every ounce of honesty and vulnerability, helped me to get to the mindset and world I live in today. It started in school, with papers where I wrote about my disorder. I was nervous at first to turn them in, but then once the first one came back with positivity, it gave me the courage to do it again. Papers turned into reports given in front of the class, which were a whole new realm of nerves and worry. Except the weird thing was, the reports didn't come with ridicule and jokes like I expected, but came with applause when I was done and acceptance. So, as you can imagine, this gave me the confidence to keep going with the topic of my own life. It was the easiest thing to write about and allowed me to let everyone know what I had.

From the papers and book reports came opportunities for people to ask me questions. My teachers, my friends, and my peers, all asked questions on multiple occasions. I loved when people asked questions because that meant that they were curious and wanted to know more. I wanted to make sure they heard it from someone living with Tourette Syndrome, and not what most people thought it to be. Curiosity also meant compassion. If someone wanted to brush me or my disorder off, then that was their problem, and they certainly wouldn't have been asking me questions. But, those teachers, friends, and students who asked more showed me there were more good people than bad. Every question motivated me to keep going.

The more my ability to believe in myself and my disorder grew, the bigger leaps of faith I would take. It was scary to put my life out there at the chance of ridicule from those around me, but it was a risk I was willing to take. I knew from a young age how important it was to be in control of my narrative. I had to put a lot of faith in the people around me and although it was scary, I'm so glad I did. Every time I chose to speak about my life, it created a new atmosphere and way of thinking in my head. It allowed me to turn this thing that could have defeated me, into one of my biggest strengths. Not only that, it became a passion in my life as I got older.

It started as wanting to share my story so that I felt like I was understood and accepted by everyone around me, but over the years, it has become so much more than that. As I got older, I realized that I didn't want people to just know my story but I wanted them to understand what it was like to live with something that takes so much away. I wanted them to know that so many other people like me existed in the world and we deserved more respect than the television and movie screen gave us. I wanted to spread awareness and education because I could tell that it needed to be spread. Most importantly, I wanted other people who were too scared or shy to share their stories to know that it was okay. That there was someone like them in the world fighting to make Tourette Syndrome known.

I'm not saying I deserve to be the "voice of Tourette Syndrome" or even that I'm trying to be. I'm just trying to make the world understand us a little better. There are so many amazing advocates out there and I'm honored to be among them. I'm trying to encourage the world to be filled with acceptance for everyone living with this disorder, or any other disability for that matter. I can't do it by myself, but my voice and every other advocate's voice will make a difference. Everyone deserves to be treated like a human being and with respect. We don't have to know someone who lives with it to spread the word. One more person who learns about Tourette Syndrome is one less joke, one less laugh, and one less child turning on the television feeling like no one cares about the struggles that they face every day. So much more needs to be done and I know I'm just one person, but they say things can have a ripple effect, and *what if* I can be a part of that ripple? What if my words *can* make a difference for someone? Some may say that's a long shot and some may say the odds are against me in making a change, but I've never been the person to back down because someone says that I can't. All that does is make me try harder and make me want it more.

It is my promise to everyone reading this book that I will never stop fighting until every single person knows what this disorder is, because one day everyone's story will be heard, the treatments will come, and the reality of this disorder will be known worldwide. I can't do it alone though, so I ask that every person reading this book, now that you know one of the many stories about a person with Tourette Syndrome—teach one other person. When you hear a joke made about the disorder, correct that person to let them know what it really is. Most importantly, find the compassion in your heart to take the time to get to know the person in front of you because that person is so much more than their disorder. It could be anyone, one of your students, colleagues, friends, or relatives. Tourette Syndrome happens, and being a source of comfort and acceptance is going to change that child's or adult's life, and I can promise you that.

Sources

Thunberg, Greta. "When Haters Go after Your Looks
and Differences, It Means They Have Nowhere
Left to Go. And Then You Know You're Winning!I
Have Aspergers and That Means I'm Sometimes a
Bit Different from the Norm. And - given the Right
Circumstances - Being Different Is a Superpow-
er.#aspiepower Pic.twitter.com/A71qVBhWUU."
Twitter. Twitter, 31 Aug. 2019. Web. 19 July
2021.

Jackson, Georgina M., Elena Nixon, and Stephen R.
Jackson. "Tic Frequency and Behavioural Measures
of Cognitive Control Are Improved in Individuals
with Tourette Syndrome by Aerobic Exercise
Training." Cortex. Elsevier, 29 Mar. 2020. Web.
22 July 2021.